A Bustle & Sew Publication

Copyright © Bustle & Sew Limited 2014

The right of Helen Dickson to be identified as the author of this work has been asserted in accordance with the Copyright, Designs and Patents Act 1988.

All rights reserved. No part of this publication may be reproduced, stored in a retrieval system or transmitted in any form, or by any means, without the prior written permission of the author, nor be otherwise circulated in any form of binding or cover other than that in which it is published and without a similar condition being imposed on the subsequent purchaser.

Every effort has been made to ensure that all the information in this book is accurate. However, due to differing conditions, tools and individual skills, the publisher cannot be responsible for any injuries, losses and other damages that may result from the use of the information in this book.

ISBN-13: 978-1500316914

ISBN-10: 1500316911

First published 2014 by:
Bustle & Sew
Coombe Leigh
Chillington
Kingsbridge
Devon TQ7 2LE
UK

www.bustleandsew.com

Hello,

And welcome to the July issue of the Bustle & Sew Magazine, full of happy summer projects for you to enjoy. At this time of year I love working with pastel cottons, deckchair stripes and floral prints, reflecting the countryside around me and the sea not so very far away.

Now is the time to take your stitching outside with you, and there are two easily portable projects, my Friendly Fox and also my first Rosie and Bear stitchery for some time. I'm thinking about a new series of Rosie & Bear designs based on old fairytales and I'd be interested to hear your thoughts about this plan.

You'll find machine applique too, as well as a Hare in a Hat, and some vintage projects to enjoy. And finally, I hope you have a lovely month of July and that the sun is shining wherever you are.

Best wishes

Helen xx

Contents

July Almanac	Page 4	Friendly Fox	Page 25
Princess and the Pea	Page 5	Strawberry Pincushions	Page 28
Some Weather Lore	Page 9	Japanese Sewing Books	Page 29
Hare in a Hat	Page 11	Bulletin Board	Page 33
Back to Basics: Needles	Page 14	Elephants in Love	Page 37
English Gardens Device Sleeve	Page 17	Making Money from Making	Page 40
Luscious Leaves	Page 20	Celebration Cake	Page 43
Vintage Loveliness	Page 22	Templates	Page 47

SUMMER

Summer is icumen in,
Lhude sing cuccu!
Groweth sed, and bloweth med,
And springth the wude nu

Anonymous c.1250

July is high summer here in the northern hemisphere, when tree canopies are in glorious full leaf, children begin their long school summer holidays and we grown-ups also head for our gardens and the great outdoors whenever weather and time allow.

In the countryside around Coombe Leigh the fields of wheat and barley are beginning to lie golden, edged with blue scabious and purple knapweed, sprinkled with glorious scarlet field poppies, whilst rosebay willowherb (wonderful name), yarrow and other wild flowers bloom in profusion in the hedgerows. There s little, if any, respite between the end of haymaking and the beginning of harvest, and it was formerly considered unlucky (or perhaps simply inconvenient!) to marry at this time: *"They that wive 'twixt sickle and scythe shall never thrive."*

The British summer has always been renowned for the unreliability of its weather, but nevertheless July and August are invariably the time of year when temperatures are at their highest. The hottest days of the year are the dog days, a period generally reckoned to last from 3 July to 11 August. This period is associated with the rising of the Dog Star (Sirius or Canicula). According to ancient superstition disease and disaster were rife at this time and dogs were at their most susceptible to rabies. In some towns and cities all dogs had to wear muzzles in public places for the duration. Of course this time of year is when the Newfies are at their sleepiest as they dislike hot sunny weather and yearn for the return of colder, damp days to come later in the year.

Ben enjoying the dog days of high summer

The USA celebrates Independence Day on the 4th July, commemorating the secession of the 13 North American colonies from Great Britain and the day is marked by public celebrations throughout the country.

Princess and the Pea

Rosie and Bear return! Princess Rosie (looking rather rumpled!) is complaining about the uncomfortable night she's endured - not a wink of sleep - due to the enormous lump in her bed. Bear, who enjoyed a lovely night's rest is handing her a magnifying glass so she can search for the (to him) non-existent object!

Shown mounted in 10" hoop

You will need:

- 12" square white cotton, linen or cotton/linen blend fabric suitable for embroidery
- 8 small scraps of printed cotton fabric, each measuring around 6" x 1". Choose scraps with a small pattern so they will look the right scale for the mattresses
- Stranded cotton floss in colours that will work well with your mattress scraps to work the blanket stitch along the bottom edges
- Also DMC stranded cotton floss in colours: 310, 321, 433, 552, 598, 729, 743, 780, 3031, 3042, 3864, 4030, blanc and Anchor stranded cotton floss in colour 1335 (Rainbow)
- Bondaweb
- 10" embroidery hoop

Applique:

- Transfer the design to the centre of your fabric using your preferred method.
- Using the reverse template trace around the mattress shapes onto the paper side of your Bondaweb. Allow a little extra on the top edge of each mattress for the overlap.
- Cut out roughly, fuse onto fabric scrap, then cut along your lines making sure you make nice long smooth cuts.
- Build up the pile of mattresses from the bottom upwards using your transferred pattern as a guide and overlapping each mattress with the one above. Fuse into place as you go.

Notes on stitching:

Use two strands of floss throughout unless otherwise stated.

Work blanket stitch along the bottom and side edges of each mattress - this helps the illusion that they're stacked on top of each other.

To stitch Bear's fur please refer to my free guide "How to Stitch Fur" which has lots of detailed notes and photographs to help you make your Bear's fur the very nicest it can be.

Just visit this link to download:

http://www.bustleandsew.com/d0wnl0ad5/rosieandbear/HowtoEmbroiderFur.pdf

When stitching his ribbon use satin stitch and change direction on the different parts of the ribbon.

Bear's eye is a couple of small stitches worked in 310 with the tiniest of tiny stitch in blanc over the top to give him a sparkle in his eye. Don't miss this stitch out as it really brings him to life.

I used Anchor stranded floss for the quilt on Rosie's bed as I particularly liked this colour combination. There is no direct DMC equivalent that I have been able to find.

Rosie's features are worked in back stitch in a single strand of 3864 and the magnifying glass which is a single strand of 310. I worked a couple of small straight stitches across the centre of the magnifying glass in 598 to represent the glass.

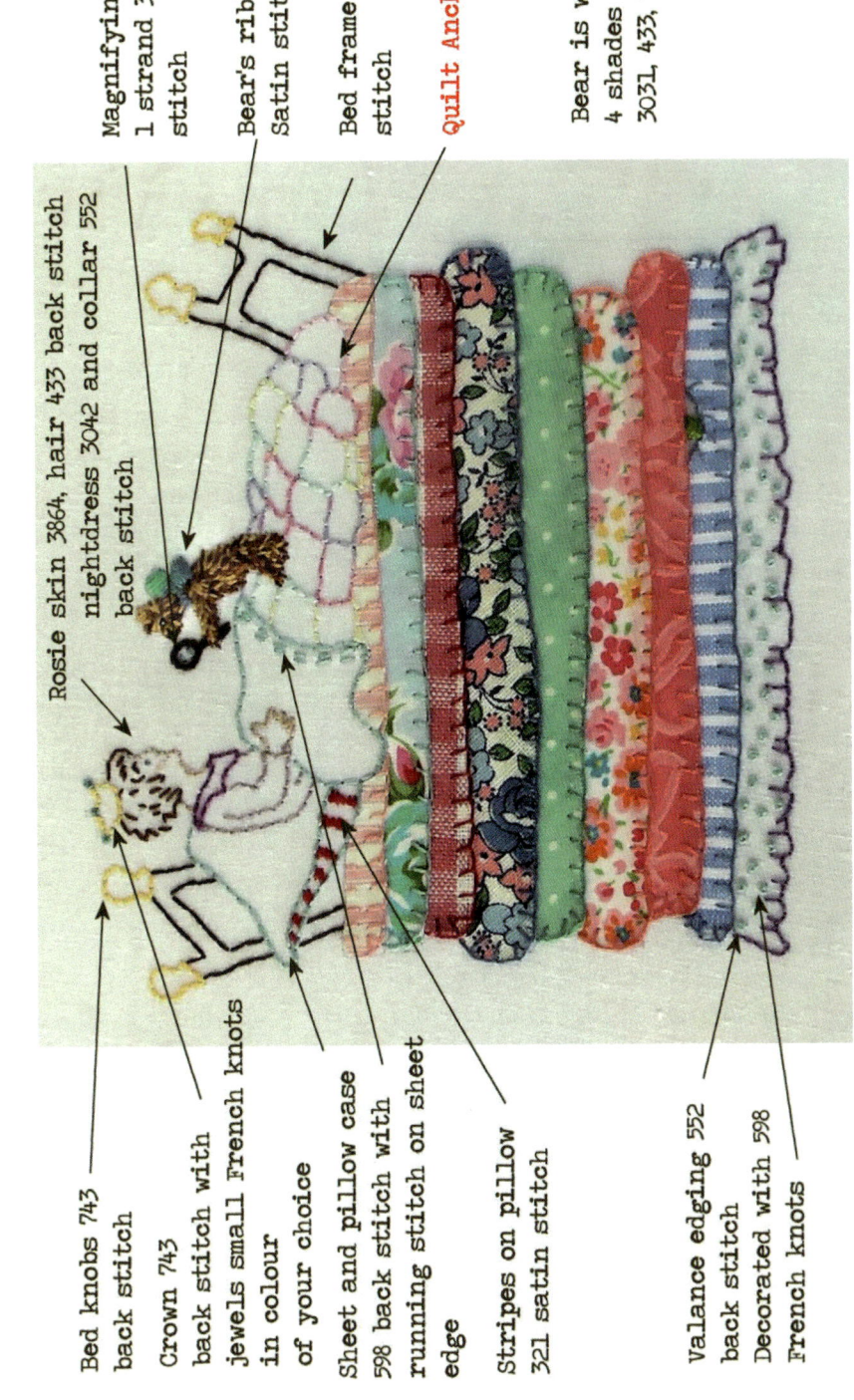

Bed knobs 743
back stitch

Crown 743
back stitch with
jewels small French knots
in colour
of your choice

Sheet and pillow case
598 back stitch with
running stitch on sheet
edge

Stripes on pillow
321 satin stitch

Valance edging 552
back stitch
Decorated with 598
French knots

Rosie skin 3864, hair 433 back stitch
nightdress 3042 and collar 552
back stitch

Magnifying glass
1 strand 310 chain
stitch

Bear's ribbon 4030
satin stitch

Bed frame 3031 back
stitch

Quilt Anchor 1335

Bear is worked in
4 shades of brown
3031, 433, 780 and 729

The Real Princess (the story of the Princess and the Pea) from the tales of Hans Christian Andersen

THERE was once a prince who wanted to marry a princess. But she must be a real princess, mind you. So he travelled all round the world, seeking such a one, but everywhere something was in the way. Not that there was any lack of princesses, but he could not seem to make out whether they were real princesses; there was always something not quite satisfactory. Therefore, home he came again, quite out of spirits, for he wished so much to marry a real princess.

One evening a terrible storm came on. It thundered and lightened, and the rain poured down; indeed, it was quite fearful. In the midst of it there came a knock at the town gate, and the old king went out to open it.

It was a princess who stood outside. But O dear, what a state she was in from the rain and bad weather! The water dropped from her hair and clothes, it ran in at the tips of her shoes and out at the heels; yet she insisted she was a real princess.

"Very well," thought the old queen; "that we shall presently see." She said nothing, but went into the bedchamber and took off all the bedding, then laid a pea on the sacking of the bedstead. Having done this, she took twenty mattresses and laid them upon the pea and placed twenty eider-down beds on top of the mattresses. The princess lay upon this bed all the night. In the morning she was asked how she had slept.

"Oh, most miserably!" she said. "I scarcely closed my eyes the whole night through. I cannot think what there could have been in the bed. I lay upon something so hard that I am quite black and blue all over. It is dreadful!"

It was now quite evident that she was a real princess, since through twenty mattresses and twenty eider-down beds she had felt the pea. None but a real princess could have such delicate feeling.

So the prince took her for his wife, for he knew that in her he had found a true princess. And the pea was preserved in the cabinet of curiosities, where it is still to be seen unless someone has stolen it. And this, mind you, is a real story.

Summer's here but will the sun shine?

A look at some Weather Lore

Here in the UK we love talking about the weather because it's nothing else if unpredictable throughout the seasons. It's not unusual to experience all four seasons in the course of a single morning - and I often walk the dogs wearing a waterproof jacket with my sunglasses in my pocket - confidently expecting to use both!

The weather in England is so changeable as we sit on the crossroads between a number of different air masses, all of which jostle for position over our heads, meaning no two days are ever the same. Hopefully by the time you read this summer really will have arrived in England - though of course nothing weather-related is certain!

Long before Admiral Robert Fitzroy, Superintendent of Britain's Meteorological Office, coined the phrase "weather forecast" in August 1861, farmers, seafarers and country folk had been relying on handed down weather lore to foretell the weather. In fact the Ancient Greeks began the science of meteorology, relating day-to-day weather to wind direction. The first weather forecaster's manual was called "On Weather Signs" and was written in the 4th century BC by Aristotle and his pupil Theophrastus.

The roots of weather lore lie in early religion and its first exponents were priests or wise men who decided the best dates for sowing and harvest. Fertility of the crops on which their survival depended meant accurate interpretation of weather signs was vital. Seafarers also became experts in weather forecasting because failure could lead to certain death - this means much of their traditional lore is very reliable. Consider "before the storm, the swell… " An oncoming gale can set up a rolling swell which travels rapidly ahead, giving warning of bad weather to come before any other indicators such as cloud and rain. I'm not quite so sure about the accuracy of their traditional belief that a new moon on a Saturday or a full one on a Sunday foretell bad weather. The combination occurring in succession is thought to be the worst sign of all.

Clouds may also indicate weather changes, "mackerel sky, twelve hours dry". This sky, dappled with small fleecy white clouds actually does mark the end of unsettled weather. Looking at the movement of upper layers of clouds can tell you of an imminent change in the weather if their direction is very different from the winds blowing the clouds beneath them. There is a famous Moroccan legend that locusts know where it will rain in the Sahara. In fact the swarms will fly downwind until they arrive at an area of converging winds, where rain is most likely.

Many country sayings about the weather haven't been scientifically proven but, based as they are on centuries of observation, are very often reliable indicators. If a candle won't light easily, or if the down flies off coltsfoot, dandelions or thistles when there is no wind, then these are signs of rain on the way. According to a rhyme said to be by the 19th century judge, Baron Charles Bowen:

"The rain it raineth every day Upon the Just and Unjust fella But more upon the Just because The Unjust stole the Just's umbrella!"

Molluscs love those rainy days!

Many people anxiously watch the weather forecast on St Swithin's Day (July 15th) for "If on St Swithin's it do rain, then forty days it will remain." Fingers crossed for a dry day on the fifteenth of this month then! American friends from Oregon told me that trees such as poplar and silver maple will turn up their leaves when it starts to rain, a fact that's well known in Europe too. The moon also features in weather lore and a well-known saying around the world is that a ring around the moon means it will rain the following day.

And finally, "when rooks build low, it's a sign of a wet summer to come". We regularly pass a large rookery on our walks up the valley and home down the old sunken bridleway. They are quieter now, but in the spring the air is full of their raucous squawks and screeches. I'm pleased to report, that this year their nests seem to be high up in the old oak trees, so am hopeful of a fine summer ahead. This isn't scientifically proven though as rooks' flight patterns are usually better weather forecasters than their nest-building habits.

Rooks are sociable birds that return to the same place year after year and because rookeries consist of many abandoned, and some renovated, old nests as well as some new ones, it's almost impossible to link nest height with the coming weather. But there is a way to forecast the weather from these comical birds. When they "tumble" through the air it's said that rain is on the way, whilst rooks that twist and turn after leaving the nest are believed to forecast storms. Weather observers give these forecasts a 70% reliability rating - which seems to me to be a lot more accurate than some of the TV or radio forecasts we all tune into so regularly.

Hare in a Hat

Mrs Hare is ready for a garden party in her beautiful summer hat! Her nose and eyes are shiny black buttons and her cheeks are blushing pink. She's easy to stitch from felt and it's fun to decorate her hat with felt flowers too.

Head measures 11" approx and is shown mounted on a 5" hoop.

You will need:

- 12" x 16" brown wool blend felt
- 8" x 4" green (or preferred colour) for hat
- 6" square lightweight printed cotton for ear inners
- Scraps of felt in flower colours, pink for cheeks and cream for eyes
- Two x ¼" black or dark brown buttons for eyes
- ¾" black or dark brown button for nose
- Dark brown or black strong thread
- Stranded cotton floss in brown and pink to match felt
- Toy stuffing
- 5" hoop
- 7" square fabric to mount head on
- Glue gun
- Pinking shears (optional)
- Long needle (optional but makes sewing eyes on much easier!)

Notes:

Apart from the dart at the back of the head the pieces are joined with wrong sides together and cross stitch using two strands of floss. Work half-cross stitch in one direction, then return in the other direction to make a nice strong seam.

Stuff the head very firmly to avoid floppiness, but don't force stuffing in or you might distort the shape.

Head:

- Cut out all pieces using templates (actual size).
- Stitch inner ears to outers as shown in picture.
- With right sides together and a short back stitch (or machine if you prefer) join the dart at the back of the head with a ⅛" seam allowance.
- Join the chin seam from base of neck to A (see template and photograph below)

- Insert gusset matching points A and X, folding ears in half vertically at base and inserting into seam as shown in diagram
- Insert back of head matching points X and B

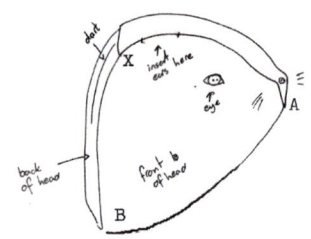

- Stuff head firmly and close at base by folding the back forward in an envelope fashion and stitching firmly.

- Sew on eyes - there's no need to stitch the cream felt shapes, they will be held in place by the buttons. Use strong thread and pull tightly to give some shape to the head.

- Sew on cheeks with two strands of pink floss and short straight stitches worked at right angles to the edges of the cheeks.

- Thread your needle with a long piece of strong thread and double it. Go into the head at one side and come out at the nose, leaving a 2" tail of thread. Make a small back stitch (it will be covered by the nose button), then come out at the other side of the nose. Leaving a loop of thread go back in and make another small back stitch at the nose. Repeat until your hare has a nice set of whiskers. Cut the loops and trim to desired length. Stitch on nose button to cover back stitches.

Make hat:

- Cut out hat base using template. Additionally cut a 4" circle from your hat felt. This will be the top of the hat.

- Make two slits in the hat base for the ears to fit through - checking carefully against your hare to make sure they're in the right place.

- With ordinary thread run a gathering thread around the edge of the 4" circle, then pull up until the top of the hat measures 2" in diameter.

- With two strands of matching embroidery floss whip stitch the gathered circle into place in the centre of the hat base.

- Turn the hat over and make a slit in the centre of the base only, then push stuffing through this slit until the crown sits up nicely. Whipstitch this opening closed.

- Cut a strip of felt 7" x ½" in a different colour to the main body and sew into place around the crown of the hat.

- Make an assortment of felt flowers from your scraps and glue them to the front of the hat. Felt flowers are really easy to make - simply cut strips of felt around ½" wide and 3" long. Cut one long side into a fringe, or a wavy shape, then just roll them up and fluff out the fringe to resemble petals. If you like you can insert a small piece of another colour of felt at the centre to represent the middle of the flower.

- When the hat's finished push onto the top of the head and if preferred glue into place with glue gun.

- Finally stretch your cotton fabric in hoop, trim of excess, fold to the inside and stick into place with your glue gun around the inside of your inner hoop.

- With glue gun glue head to the fabric. The head is quite light so you won't need to sew or wire it at all, and you don't need cardboard to reinforce the fabric either. Your hare is now finished.

Back to Basics
Your Needle

The needles we use today have come a long way since the first days of sewing when thorns or fish bones were used to stitch two pieces of fabric together. Steel needles were introduced in the 16th century and have become finer as technological advances have been made in their manufacture. There are a range of types, sizes and gauges available to us today which have all been developed for specific uses.

Using the right needle for the task in hand will make your work so much quicker and easier. Be sure to keep your needles safely in a needlebook as they can easily blunt if you leave them rattling around loose in a box or tin.

The following are the kinds those you're most likely to come across:

Crewel

Crewel or embroidery needles have a sharp point and a long eye that allows you to thread many strands.

Tapestry

Used for cross stitch or other work on canvas, aida and evenweave fabric. They have blunt ends so they can pass through your work without splitting the fabric threads.

Chenille

Similar to a tapestry needle, but with a sharp point to pieces the fabric, a chenille needle is useful for stitching with textured yarns.

Sharps

These are all-purpose needles with easy-to-thread eyes. They're available in 12 sizes, but the most generally useful are sizes 6 to 9.

Beading

Beading needles are fine and flexible so they can easily go through the holes in even the tiniest beads and are able to hold several beads at once.

Darning

Strong and sturdy with a large eye and blunt end, these needles are easy to thread with wool and to thread in and out of the weave of a woollen fabric.

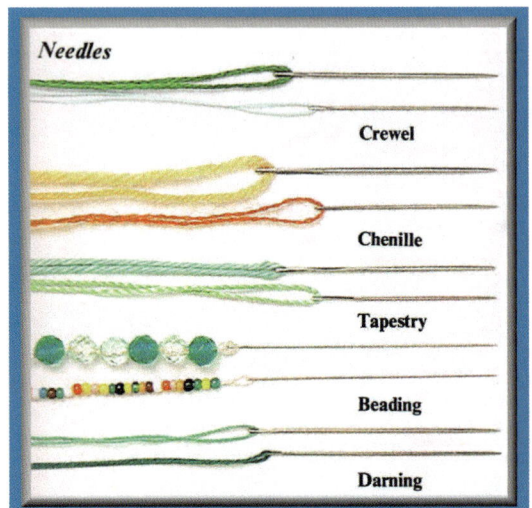

> Hand sewing needles come in 10 sizes from No.1 (very heavy) to No.12 (very fine).

Don't economise on needles, but choose the best quality you can find. The eyes of cheap needles are often imperfectly drilled; the hole may be rough or incomplete which will fray your floss - or maybe it won't go through at all. If your needle bends (though it shouldn't if it's a good one), discard it immediately as you can't stitch neatly with a crooked needle.

Remember always to use the right needle for your work - both for floss and fabric. If you choose a needle whose eye is too small it will roughen and fray your floss and be hard to pull through your work. On the other hand, it's nearly as bad to have too large a needle as your stitches will look horrible if the needle makes holes in the fabric larger than your floss can fill.

Threading your needle

Loop Method

Loop the end of your thread over the eye of your needle and pinch it tightly together

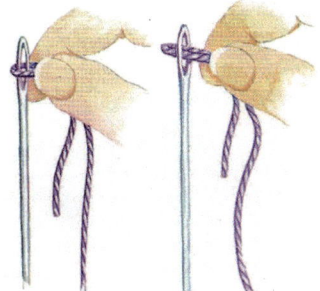

Slip the pinched loop off the needle and push the fold of the thread through the eye of the needle.

Paper Method

Cut a strip of paper that's narrow enough to fit through the eye of your needle. Fold it in half over the end of the thread, Push the paper through the needle eye, pulling your thread with it.

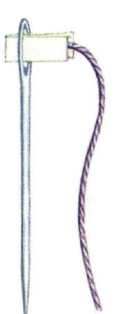

Needle Threader

These are often sold with packets of needles. To use one, slip the wire loop of the needle threader through the eye of your needle. Place your thread through the loop and pull the threader back out through the needle eye, bringing your thread with it.

And finally … metallic threads can be *sooo* frustrating to sew with - try this method for threading your needle with metallics:

Loop the end of the thread and push through the eye of the needle. Pass over the needle point and pull in order to tighten the loop and secure your thread. Threading metallics in this way will help prevent them from shredding as you stitch.

English Gardens Device Sleeve

Make your device really girly with this 1930s inspired applique cover. Machine stitched applique makes the cover really hardwearing, whilst the ladybird and bumble bee add that unique Bustle & Sew touch!

Includes how to measure your device to ensure your sleeve fits perfectly.

To determine the sizing for your device, you will need to measure it:

Once you have these measurements you can determine your pattern size. You will need to cut two large fabric pieces for the exterior and two for the interior. Each will measure (length + height + 1)" x (width + height +1)" : the extra 1" is for seam allowances of ¼" and ease.

If you are using wadding, then cut both your interior fabric and wadding ½" smaller than your exterior. If, like me, you are using felted woollen or other thick soft fabric, then there is no need to adjust the interior measurements at this stage - if the fit is too tight, then you can adjust seam allowances slightly on the interior if necessary.

You will need:

- 2 pieces of plain medium weight fabric for exterior
- 2 pieces of felted wool/thick wool felt/blanket or other soft thick fabric for interior. You may use a light-weight fabric and include wadding if preferred.
- 6" narrow ribbon or tape
- 1" button
- 5" square fabric for pocket at back (optional) Assorted felt and fabric scraps for applique
- Tiny amounts red, black, yellow, grey and ivory stranded cotton embroidery floss
- Bondaweb
- Embroidery foot for your sewing machine and dark thread for the needle
- Temporary fabric marker pen

Applique:

- Transfer the design at the end to one of your exterior pieces, positioning it about 1 ¼" up from the bottom edge and centrally vertically.
- Working from the bottom up, trace your applique shapes onto the paper side of your Bondaweb, then press to the fabric of your choice, cut out and position. Secure in place by ironing when you're happy with the position. Pay attention to how some of the pieces overlap - I find it easiest to work from the bottom of the design upwards.
- Fit the embroidery foot to your sewing machien and secure each applique piece in place with two lines of machine stitching using a scribble effect.
- With your temporary fabric marker pen draw lines for veins of leaves and stalks then work veins in two lines and stalks in several lines o stitching. Remember you're aiming for a scribbled effect - not too neat - as though you'd roughly outlined the pieces with pencil.
- When the machine applique is finished add the little bee and ladybird by hand if you'd like.

Ladybirds:

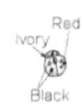

Use a single strand of floss. Work the back in red satin stitch in two sections lengthwise. Work the head crosswise in black satin stitch. Make two stitches down the back of the ladybird for the edge of the wing cases and work 4 French knots with only one twist in each knot. Add two single twist French knots in ivory for eyes.

Bumble Bee:

Use a single strand of floss. Work body in satin stitch as shown and legs in straight stitch. Wings are detached chain stitch.

Press your work lightly on the reverse and set to one side.

Exterior Back:

- Take your 5" square of fabric and fold under ½" all the way round. Top stitch top edge, then position on back 3" up from bottom edge and centrally vertically. Top stitch around three sides leaving the top edge open to form a patch pocket. This is useful for your headphones etc.

Assemble Sleeve:

- To make exterior place together and stitch around all edges with a ¼" seam allowance. Trim corners. Turn right side out.

- Complete interior as exterior, but leave a 3" gap in the centre of the bottom to turn through.

- Place interior inside exterior, right sides together. Match side seams and pin or tack together around top edge. Fold narrow ribbon in half and position in centre of front edge with ends of ribbon matching raw edges of fabric. Stitch all around top edge.

- Trim and turn right side out through gap in bottom. Topstitch gap closed. Turn sleeve right side out and push lining down inside. Press and topstitch around top edge for a neat finish. Position button and stitch to back.

Salads are wonderful at this time of year - it's salad with everything as far as I'm concerned - and if you decide to grow your own salad leaves - which isn't hard to do, then you'll be able to serve wonderful bowls of deliciousness all summer through - beating supermarket produce hands–down in terms of freshness and flavour. There's nothing quite so nice as the taste of leaves that were still growing just a few hours before you eat them, and the wonderful fresh aroma of a newly picked lettuce has long since disappeared by the time it's been packed in plastic and transported across the country.

If you have the space, then salad leaves are easy to grow - and even if your garden is small, it's worth trying cut and come again varieties, or choose something a little unusual that's hard (or expensive) to obtain in the shops. Many of the more unusual salad leaves, for example, can only be purchased in expensive mixed packs, and you may also not be too keen on the fact that they're washed in chlorine bleach and packed in special gas to help them keep longer.

Cos lettuce is widely available but lettuces are often heavily sprayed with pesticides - that's the reason you often see just the hearts on sale. In my mind that alone makes them worth allocating space for. For colour why not try russet-red "Lollo Rosso" or some red oak leaf lettuce perhaps? The leaves of "Flame" turn cherry red in the centre as they grow whilst those of "Pablo" are overlaid with dark purple. If you like a slightly bitter tang in your salad then grow radicchio, chicory and endive.

Rocket is expensive to buy, but actually grows very fast and is extremely tolerant regarding position and soil type. It's a hardy annual and can withstand a mild winter. Pick the leaves whilst they're young and, as it will run to seed quickly in hot weather, sew it frequently in small quantities.

You don't often see leaf sorrel for sale here in the UK and that's a pity as its lemony flavour makes a great addition to any salad. It's incredibly easy to grow and, as a bonus, also makes fabulous soup.

Try also some oriental vegetables - largely unknown on the British table 20 years ago. Pak choi is delicious raw in salads, as well as steamed, braised or stir fried, whilst mizuna will grow in both summer and winter, its pretty foliage adding a decorative touch.

Oriental brassicas don't like their roots to be disturbed and are more shallow-rooted than the typical British brassicas so be sure to keep them well watered. It's best to sew them directly into position or else in modules to avoid root disturbance. You can expect to be eating pak choi within about six weeks of planting whilst mizuna should be ready in about ten weeks.

Whatever you decide to plant I hope you have a happy summer of both growing and eating your own salad leaves - delicious and healthy too!

Luscious Leaves .....

Some Vintage Loveliness

On my shelf upstairs I have a collection of vintage sewing books, many of which used to belong to my grandmothers, both of whom were keen needlewomen, including the book above from which this idea for making dolls' clothes is taken.

I remember sitting with my grandma and making a dress for my teddy bear from these exact pages, though I don't think we worried too much about he rest of the outfit! Like Rosie and her Bear, I still have my furry childhood friend - though my bear is called Sunshine as she was originally covered in glorious golden mohair fur, though this was worn away in patches by too much love. Sadly I don't have my teddy bear's dress any more, though I remember it as being a rather pretty pink.

EMBROIDERY WITH A PRACTICAL APPLICATION

THE CHILD. Elizabeth Anne had been dreaming again—one of those irritating dreams (when remembered afterwards) in which everything had been exactly what she longed to possess. There had been a doll, for instance—— As a matter of fact, Elizabeth Anne had a doll, a perfectly good new one, but evidently the sum allotted to the purchase by the kind donor had covered only the doll itself and left her garmentless in a world where the prejudice is all in favour of clothing.

Luckily, Auntie Grace came to tea that afternoon and having found out the cause of Anne's absent-mindedness came to the rescue with a suggestion that they should make some doll's clothes.

"Can you draw a circle?" she asked. Of course Elizabeth Anne had learned to do that at school, so paper, compass, and pencils were procured and laid on the nursery table together with pins, needles, scissors, some skeins of bright blue, green, gold, white and scarlet embroidery cotton and a length of ravishing scarlet material which Mummy had bought at the sales and was now glad to find a use for.

Elizabeth Anne was almost too excited to draw, but with Auntie's help she drew a circle for the skirt on the paper and inside it, a smaller circle. Then a small circle to be halved, for the cape-sleeves. Auntie then drew the little shape for the bodice which you will find in the drawing *No. 51*. These shapes were all cut out of the paper and then from the scarlet cloth.

the edge of sleeves and lower armhole finished with blanket stitch in blue embroidery cotton. The foot of the skirt was also blanket-stitched with blue and two inches up from the front was put a row of herring-bone stitch in green. The neck was turned in with a narrow edge hemmed in Elizabeth Anne's best stitches and decorated with a row of herring-bone stitch in blue.

Auntie now took a penny and drew three circles to form a small group of daisies like the sketch *No. 55*, and added a few stems. Elizabeth Anne was shown how to button-stitch those; one in blue, one in white, one in gold and the centres in French knots. The stems she embroidered with chain stitch in green.

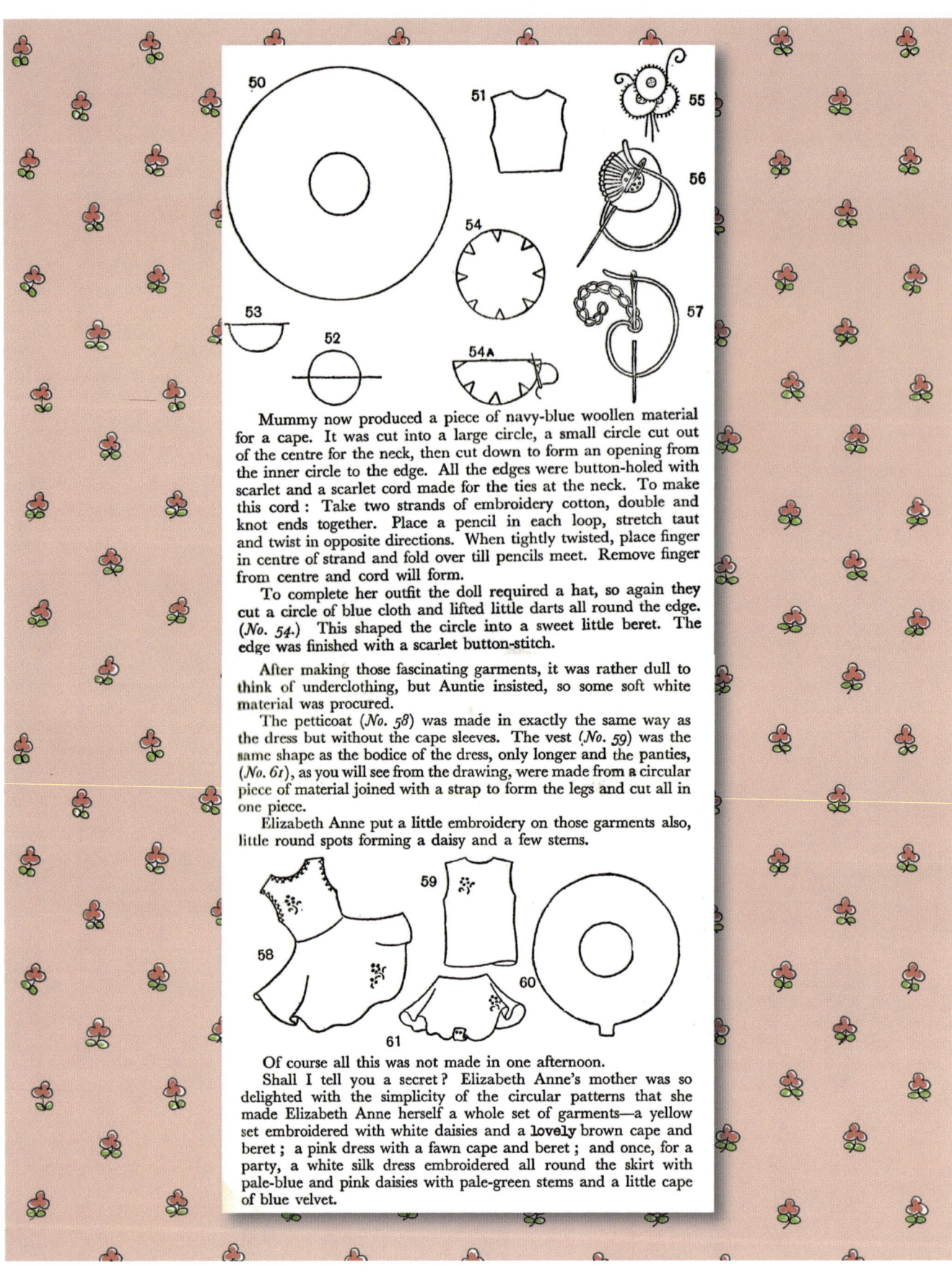

Mummy now produced a piece of navy-blue woollen material for a cape. It was cut into a large circle, a small circle cut out of the centre for the neck, then cut down to form an opening from the inner circle to the edge. All the edges were button-holed with scarlet and a scarlet cord made for the ties at the neck. To make this cord: Take two strands of embroidery cotton, double and knot ends together. Place a pencil in each loop, stretch taut and twist in opposite directions. When tightly twisted, place finger in centre of strand and fold over till pencils meet. Remove finger from centre and cord will form.

To complete her outfit the doll required a hat, so again they cut a circle of blue cloth and lifted little darts all round the edge. (*No. 54.*) This shaped the circle into a sweet little beret. The edge was finished with a scarlet button-stitch.

After making those fascinating garments, it was rather dull to think of underclothing, but Auntie insisted, so some soft white material was procured.

The petticoat (*No. 58*) was made in exactly the same way as the dress but without the cape sleeves. The vest (*No. 59*) was the same shape as the bodice of the dress, only longer and the panties, (*No. 61*), as you will see from the drawing, were made from a circular piece of material joined with a strap to form the legs and cut all in one piece.

Elizabeth Anne put a little embroidery on those garments also, little round spots forming a daisy and a few stems.

Of course all this was not made in one afternoon.

Shall I tell you a secret? Elizabeth Anne's mother was so delighted with the simplicity of the circular patterns that she made Elizabeth Anne herself a whole set of garments—a yellow set embroidered with white daisies and a **lovely** brown cape and beret; a pink dress with a fawn cape and beret; and once, for a party, a white silk dress embroidered all round the skirt with pale-blue and pink daisies with pale-green stems and a little cape of blue velvet.

Friendly Fox Embroidery

"Nothing's nicer than a friend"

Show your friends how much you appreciate them with this endearing little fox and his best friend the bluebird. Really easy embroidery and a little applique make this a great beginner's project or a quick make for the more experienced.

Shown mounted in a 7" hoop.

You will need:

- 10" square white fabric suitable for embroidery
- Scraps of brown, cream and blue fabric for applique
- DMC stranded cotton floss in colours: 310, 321, 604, 794, 823, 905, 906, ecru, a brown colour to match the fabric you have chosen for the fox's body and a blue to match the bird's body
- Bondaweb
- 7" embroidery hoop
- ¾" wide strips of fabric (torn into strips rather than cut) and glue gun to attach to hoop if you want to bind your hoop to display. Alternatively you could leave plain or paint.

Method:

- Transfer design to fabric using preferred method. The pattern is given actual size and also in reverse to suit your preferred method of transfer.
- Using the reversed pattern trace the applique shapes onto the paper side of your Bondaweb. The cream markings sit on top of the main body piece so allow a little extra on the end of the tail for the tip to overlap - and cut away a little more on the bottom of the chin.
- Cut out shapes roughly and fuse to the reverse of your fabric, then cut out carefully using long smooth scissor strokes to avoid ragged edges. Position on fabric and iron into place when happy with the positioning.
- Secure the shapes to the background using two strands of matching floss and small straight stitches worked at right-angles to the edges of the applique pieces.
- Work embroidery as shown on stitch guide using two strands of floss throughout. When finished press lightly on the reverse.

Wrap hoop:

- To wrap your hoop take the screw out. With your glue gun dot a little glue on the bottom edge of the wooden hoop and secure one end of a ¾" strip of fabric to the hoop. Wrap around the hoop, overlapping slightly as you go to ensure complete coverage, beginning and ending strips at the back of the hoop - cutting your strips if necessary.
- When finished reinsert screw and mount work in frame. Trim fabric to less than 1" all the way around and glue to the inside of the inner hoop. If preferred you can cover the back of the work with a circle of white or cream felt for a nice neat finish.

Eyes 310
Bird tiny straight stitch
Fox French knot with a tiny ecru stitch for sparkle

Heart and flower buds 321 satin stitch

Tulips and flower centres 794 satin stitch

Text 823 back stitch

Leaves satin stitch and stalks back stitch dark green 906 and light green 905

Flower petals 604 satin stitch

A Pin Cushion for Mother

MATERIALS

Red cotton cloth	Thread
Cotton	Darning needle
Green yarn	Scissors

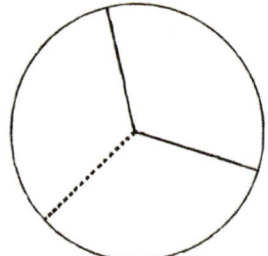

1. To make a paper pattern, cut out a circle 6" in diameter. Divide into thirds. One third of the circle makes the pattern.

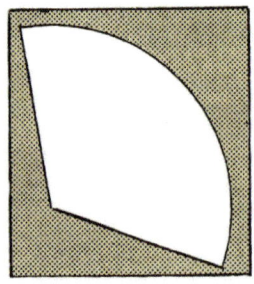

2. Pin the pattern on red cotton cloth and cut around it.

3. Fold and sew with fine stitches along straight edges.

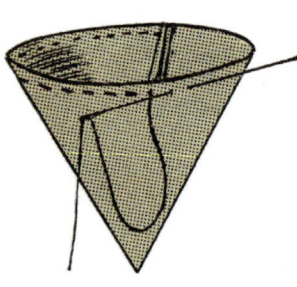

4. Turn so the seam is inside and sew a gathering stitch about 1/4" from top.

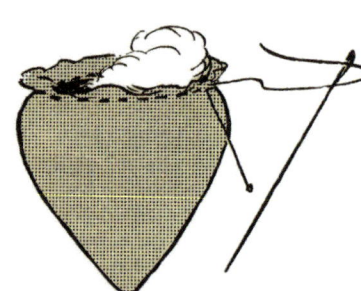

5. Fill with cotton.

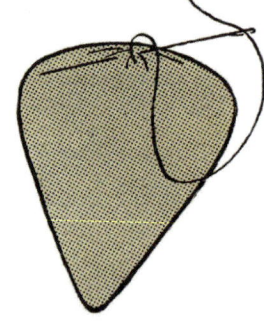

6. Pull top together. Tuck raw edge of cloth in and fasten thread securely.

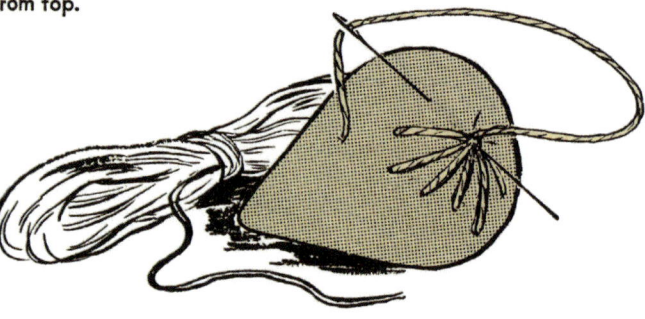

7. Make long stitches with green yarn and finish with a loop of yarn in center. Stick pins into pin cushion to simulate the speckled surface of a strawberry.

TURNING JAPANESE

.... a look at Japanese craft books

Japanese craft books hold the key to a world of wonderful creating - and you don't need to understand the language to join in!

Over the last year or two I've become a huge fan of Japanese pattern books with their beautiful photography and simple, uncluttered layout they're fantastic eye-candy as well as a source of inspiration and simple designs to stitch when I'm in a hurry to create something special.

I have a small, but increasing, library of Japanese embroidery, patchwork and toy-making books, though I've never felt brave enough to dip into crochet and knitting. I think if I were a better crocheter, able to read those funny patterns with all the lines heading off in different directions then I'd give it a go … but I'm not at all sure about understanding knitting patterns at all, though oddly I have no problem in following knitting charts. Although maybe that's not so odd, I have after all been knitting for (ahem!) over 40 years!!

So I have restricted myself to Japanese sewing books – which is absolutely no hardship at all. As well as being beautiful to look at, they're also very practical guides and, even though everything is written in Japanese, they're surprisingly easy to use. The images and patterns are so clearly laid out that even the illiterate (in Japanese!) user will find it

quite straightforward to assemble a project, often with less confusion than when following a pattern written in English. And of course if you're simply using an embroidery design, then very few instructions at all are needed!

The typical layout of a Japanese pattern book is for the first part to consist of beautiful photographs of the finished project, each carefully numbered (in our own numerals) for reference. If you're using an embroidery book then you'll often see a stitch guide for the more unfamiliar stitches or unusual techniques. Again these are well-illustrated and normally you shouldn't have any problem in following the step-by-step pictures. The back part of the book is the instructions – just turn to the page with the number of the pattern you want to make and you'll find the following information:

- A very clear line drawing – or sometimes a photograph of all the constituent parts of the project

- Step by step diagrams showing each stage of assembling the project, demonstrating in detail if there are any trickier steps such as inserting a zip

Embroidery books however don't follow this layout – you usually see a double-spread of completed stitching, followed by the patterns on the next two pages. This is great as you don't need to flick backwards and forwards through the book to find the right pattern for your design. Stitches and floss colours are written in Japanese, but it's usually possible to work these out by closely studying the photographs of the finished designs. And if you can't … then just substitute your own ideas – after all that's part of the fun!

But if you are making a project that requires assembly, you'll find the actual pattern pieces at the back of the book, normally all printed together on a large, double-sided, easy-to-remove sheet of thick paper. When you unfold it at first it will just appear to be a mess of different coloured lines with strange Japanese characters dotted around. But don't panic –

take a deep breath and a moment or two to study it more closely.

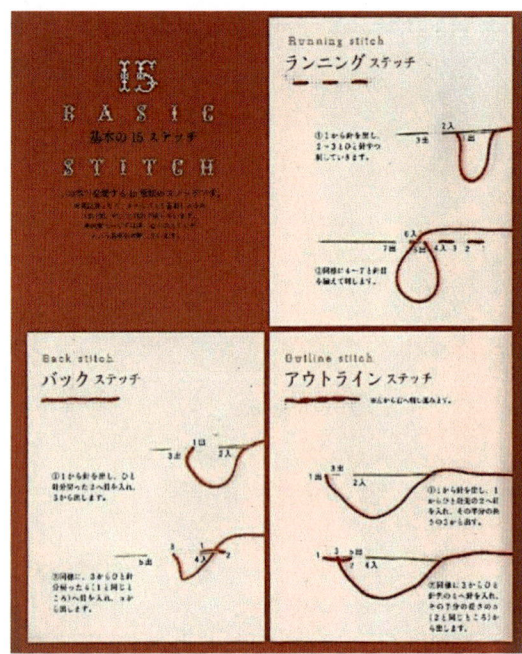

The first step is to look for the number of the project you want to make (the one displayed next to the project photograph at the front of the book). Once you've identified this, then look at the lines closely, they're sometimes, but not always printed in different colours – I often like to draw over the pattern lines I'm using with a coloured marker pen to make it clearer before I trace the pattern itself onto tissue paper. I find this helps focus my thoughts on all the pieces, and consider carefully how they will fit together from the beginning to end of my project.

I don't have any Japanese at all, but have learned to recognise a few basic symbols, though even this isn't necessary to be able to use these books effectively. It's so simple to follow the pictures and no written explanation is usually necessary – and it does help that project titles and numerals are generally included in our own alphabet so you always have a point of reference.

Japanese pattern books are surprisingly easy to find these days… and I would recommend the following Etsy shops (they're not UK based and although shipping does add to the price, my books have always arrived in super-fast time).

Pomadour's Craft Café   Wonderful Etsy shop with a fantastic range of craft books. A small range of supplies, including fabric, and some Japanese goods too.

https://www.etsy.com/shop/pomadour24

Pink Nelie Another Etsy shop with a good range of craft books. Super-fast international shipping.

https://www.etsy.com/uk/shop/PinkNelie

M is for Make UK-based site – nice selection of fabrics, also some craft books (dressmaking only)

http://www.misformake.co.uk/

If you're a fan of Japanese Craft books and have your own favourite sources, then please do let me know so I can share with other readers. Thanks!!

Oh .. and the term "zakka" which you'll often find used to describe these books – what does it mean? I didn't know either, though I'm familiar with the look. So I searched online and this is what I found.. (thanks Wikipedia)

"Zakka (from the Japanese 'zak-ka'□ or 'many things') is a fashion and design phenomenon that has spread from Japan throughout Asia. The term refers to everything and anything that improves your home, life and appearance. It is often based on household items from the West that are regarded as kitsch in their countries of origin, but it can also be Japanese goods, mainly from the fifties, sixties, and seventies. In Japan there are also so-called Asian zakka stores; that usually refers to Southeast Asia. The interest in Nordic design or Scandinavian design, both contemporary and past, is also part of this zakka movement. Zakka can also be contemporary handicraft.

Zakka has also been described as "the art of seeing the savvy in the ordinary and mundane". The zakka boom could be recognized as merely another in a series of consumer fads, but it also touches issues of self-expression and spirituality. "Cute, corny and kitschy is not enough. To qualify as a zakka, a product must be attractive, sensitive, and laden with subtext."

RAIN

The rain is raining all around

It falls on field and tree

It rains on the umbrellas here

And on the ships at sea

R L Stevenson "A Child's Garden of Verses"

Bulletin Board

Here's a quick project with a bit of a difference - not too much sewing, but a great way to use up assorted bits and pieces you may have lying around.

Take an old picture frame, some wadding, and a few buttons - as well as your prettiest fabric to create a lovely item for your home - and unlike many ideas for making these boards - not a single hammer, tack or piece of chipboard in sight!

My picture frame was a standard European A3 size, roughly 12" x 16" and so I'll give details for these dimensions. Simply adjust if you're using a differently sized frame.

You will need:

- 12" x 16" picture frame
- 12" x 16" piece polyester batting
- 16" x 20" piece light or medium weight non-stretchy fabric (I used half an Ikea tea towel!)
- 15 yards x 3/8" (1 cm) wide ribbon
- 18 small (around 3/8") buttons
- PVA craft glue
- Brown parcel tape
- Fabric spray adhesive
- Embroidery floss in a colour that works well with your background fabric

Method:

- Disassemble your frame and dispose of the glass safely. At this stage I painted my frame as it was a dark wood. I used ordinary satin wood paint, one coat of primer and one of topcoat in a soft grey.

- Lay your fabric on a clean flat surface and place the top of the frame in the centre. With a temporary fabric marker pen draw around the inside of the frame to indicate the part of the fabric that will be visible when your project is finished. Measure and mark 4" intervals along the sides.

- Attach the polyester batting to the reverse of your fabric using fabric spray adhesive, ensuring it is centred on your fabric.

- Position ribbon in a criss-cross pattern across the fabric, cutting into strips as you go, meeting at the marks you made along the sides. Pin at the edges.

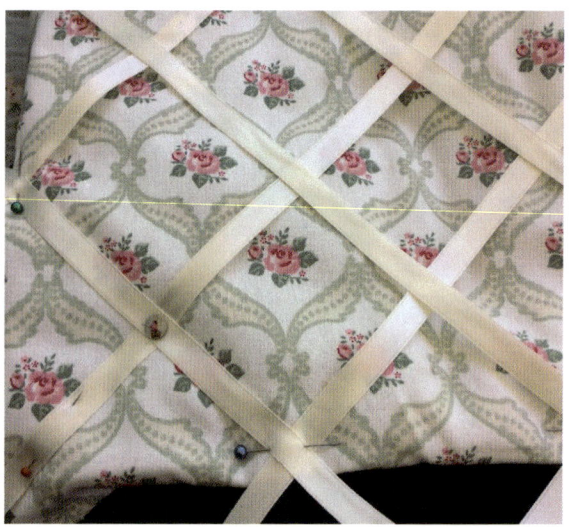

- Where two strips cross secure into place with a button stitched with embroidery floss through both the fabric and batting. Pull the floss fairly tightly.

- Lay the frame backing on a clean flat surface with the interior side uppermost. Coat with PVA glue.

- Place your bulletin board fabric right side up on top and press down to firmly adhere the batting to the picture frame back. Leave until completely dry.

- When dry place face down and fold the extra fabric to the back of the picture frame. Pull until taut but not tight and secure in place with brown parcel tape. Do the two long sides first and then the two short sides.

- When the ribbons are secured machine stitch along the line you drew earlier that indicates the inside of the frame. This will hold the edges firm. (In the picture below you'll notice I actually went around twice, but with hindsight I don't think this is necessary)

- Trim away excess fabric at the corners to avoid extra bulk.

- Insert bulletin board front into frame and if your frame has them press down tabs to secure (most ready-made frames have these, if not you may need to insert pins or staples) Cover edges with a second layer of parcel tape. If you liked you could finish with wallpaper or wrapping paper for a pretty back, but I didn't do this.

- Your bulletin board is now finished.

Don't forget to download your FREE e-book from Bustle & Sew.

CLICK HERE for the pdf file.

http://bustleandsew.com/freepatterns/SimpleStitcheryPrimer.pdf

Elephants in Love Applique

Cute little applique elephants sitting in rows, and just two who have fallen for each other! Easy to create applique.

A great project for beginners or a quick easy make for the more experienced.

This pattern makes a cushion cover for an 18" (45 cm) pad. It has a simple envelope closure at the back. It is sized to be slightly smaller than the pad as this allows for compression of the pad with time so the cushion should stay plump. If you want it to be larger than the pad for a flatter cushion then simply add an additional ½" (1cm) seam allowance all the way round.

You will need:

- Base fabric for front panel- medium weight un-patterned cotton, linen or woollen fabric, must not be stretchy. 1 piece 18" (45cm) square,
- Fabric for back panel - same as above but may be patterned if desired. 2 pieces 18" (45 cm) x 12" (30 cm)
- 6" (15 cm) square wool blend felt in mid-blue
- 6" (15 cm) square wool blend felt in pink
- 6" (15 cm) square wool blend felt in light blue
- 3" (6 cm) square wool blend felt in red
- 8 x 4" (10 cm) square pieces of patterned cotton or linen (why not use scraps from much loved clothes that are no longer worn?)
- 1 skein stranded cotton floss in aqua 1
- skein stranded cotton floss in damson
- 18" (45 cm) square cushion pad
- Temporary fabric spray adhesive

Seam allowance is ¼"

Complete front applique panel:

- Cut out your elephants. You will need 8 elephants facing to the left - cut these from your patterned fabric.
- Cut out your elephants. You will need 8 elephants facing to the left - cut these from your patterned fabric.
- Cut out 4 elephant ears from pink felt and 4 elephant ears from light blue felt
- Now cut one elephant facing right from mid-blue felt. To do this simply reverse your template. Cut one elephant ear from light blue felt for the right-facing elephant. To do this simply reverse your template.

- Take your front panel
- Fold into 3 equal parts lengthways and press lightly along folds.
- Open out and then fold into 3 equal parts widthways and press lightly along folds.
- Open out your pad. It will now be divided into 9 equal squares along the folds. This will help you position your elephants.

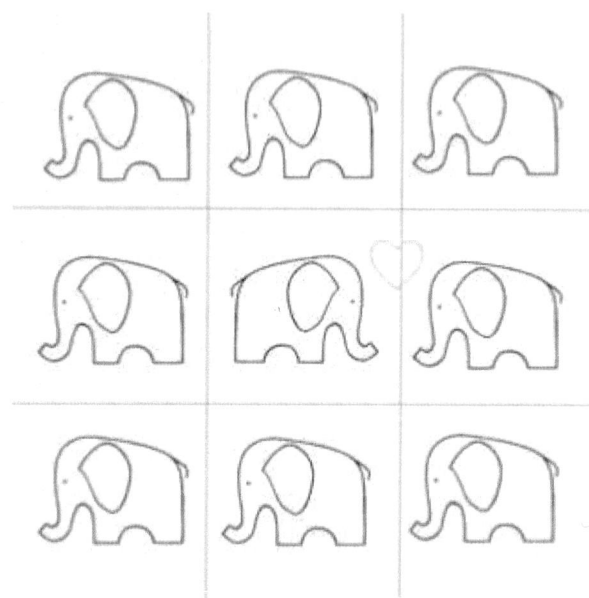

- Position your elephants. (see above) Play around a little until you are happy with the way they look. The light blue, right-facing elephant must be in the middle square.
- Fix your elephants with temporary spray adhesive. Apart from the centre elephant, position each elephant slightly off centre of the square, towards the centre of the cushion. (This is to allow for the seam allowance around the edges of the panel).
- Fix the elephants' ears with spray adhesive. Randomly mix the pink and blue ears apart from the centre elephant whose ear is blue.

- Position the felt heart. It is slightly off the fold so it will be equally spaced between the elephants (remember you positioned the right-hand elephant a little more towards the centre).

- Straight stitch over the edges of the elephants' ears keeping each stitch at right-angles to the edge of the ear.

- Blanket stitch around the elephant shapes using 3 strands of aqua floss.

  - Straight stitch around the edge of the heart using 3 strands of damson floss.

  - Work a single cross-stitch for each elephant's eye using 6 strands of damson floss.

  - Work 2 straight stitches and one lazy daisy stitch for each tail using the template as a guide to position your stitches.

  - Press lightly on reverse.

Assemble your cushion:

- Take your two smaller pieces of base fabric (it can look effective to make these in a patterned fabric to give interest to the back of the cushion). These pieces will form the back of the pillow.

- Hem each piece along one of the longer sides. (If you're using a patterned fabric be sure to take the direction of the pattern into account). Press hems.

- Lay your applique front panel on your work surface right side facing up.

- Lay the two back pieces on top of the front panel with the right sides of the fabric facing down. Line up the un-hemmed 18" (45 cm) edge of the first back piece along one side of the front panel. Line up the un-hemmed 18" (45 cm) of the second back piece along the other side of the front panel.

- Pin or tack your pieces in place.

- Machine stitch together around the edges Make the corners rounded rather than square, especially if using a woollen fabric as this will make them neater once turned. (I usually go around twice for extra strength!)

- Clip seams with pinking shears to minimize fraying or overstitch with your machine.

- Turn right side out. Insert cushion pad.

FINISHED!

Making Money from Making

We've already talked about using traditional marketing methods to promote your business - but now that you have an online presence it's important to consider how you'll attract visitors to your Facebook page, blog or Etsy/Folksy shop. It's well-known that word of mouth is one of the most effective sales tools for all businesses, large or small. We tend to trust our family and friends when they tell us something is good - after all we value their opinions! Social media is simply a way of harnessing this word of mouth effect and expanding it to reach thousands of new potential customers. People using social media tend to share the same likes and interests as other members of their social networks and, in the same way as family and friends, are likely to value their opinions and advice.

Today it's important that any business, large or small, has a strong online presence and, with just a little time and effort, social media marketing can be the most cost-effective form of marketing you ever undertake.

Facebook (FB)

You may or may not have a personal FB account already and if you don't you will need to set one up. This is really easy to do and FB guide you through the process. You have to have a personal account as FB require that to use their site you provide your real name and personal information. But don't worry, none of this will be visible to anyone unless you choose to share it. And your business page will be totally separate to your personal account so users of your business page won't e able to access your personal information, be your friend or even know that it was you who created the page.

Last month I mentioned the need to choose your page name carefully, ensuring that your business name is part of the web address. To some extent you can customise your page's appearance to fit in with your business brand and can also include links to your shop/blog or other places you'd like people to visit.

Once your page is set up and ready to go, then you'll need to attract visitors. Business pages on FB now have "likers" - which is exactly what it says - people who know about your business and like it! Your page will need to have likers in order to have any impact at all - and it's fair to say that to get likers you will need to be likeable (sure this won't be a problem!) When people visit your page they'll want to find quality content and active engagement with others. If you already have a FB account then share your page with your current FB friends and family - if they won't support your best efforts, then who will? It's important to encourage two-way interaction on your page so that people want to return to catch up with the latest developments. Here are some top tips for doing this:

- Post questions - ask for people's opinion on something, whether it's the best stitch to use in a particular project, their favourite colour combinations or even something as silly as what the weather's doing today - you'll be amazed at some of the responses you'll receive. I'm continually blown away by what a witty, articulate *fun* collection of people I am lucky enough to have visit my page.

- Write concise, informative, updates on business developments Post links to relevant websites - have you discovered a great new fabric source? Then share it with others who might be interested.

- Post images and perhaps consider uploading videos - a walk you enjoyed? A craft fair or stately home you visited?

- And above all, reply to comments to show you've read them and value the time and trouble taken to leave them

Once your page is up and running, then consider posting on other pages and forums related to your work where you'll "meet" likeminded people and encourage them to visit your page and perhaps in time become your customers. One of the key benefits of FB is the way that you can share with other people. If someone "likes" your page it will appear in their feed and be seen by their friends, some of whom will like it too - so it will be seen by their friends - and so on …..
This is what drives more visitors and potential customers to your page.

Twitter

Twitter is another potential means of attracting customers - it is a social networking and micro-blogging service that originally launched around 8 years ago. It enables users to send and receive messages known as "tweets". These are text-based posts of up to 140 characters that are displayed on the user's profile page. Users can follow each other, forward - or retweet - other people's messages and easily chat to one another. If you decide to use Twitter to raise your PR profile, then make sure to follow magazines, websites and other media appropriate to your business as they almost always tweet about upcoming features and input they're seeking.

Don't fall into the trap of just telling people about your business - remember that you're chatting to other people, not giving a lecture. Interact and engage with your followers and the people you follow, showing that you're interested in what they're doing. Remember that your language and responses will influence people's perception of you and your brand. Indeed, tweeting too much about your business will look like spam and people will quickly lose interest.

Blogging

Blogging is also a great way to engage with people, but only if you enjoy writing and are willing to commit to keeping your blog up to date. You should aim to post a minimum of one article a week, but more is good, though this will depend on the amount of time you have available and the topics you want to cover. When blogging in particular, remember that the information you post can, and probably will, be read by people across the globe so if you're not writing exclusively about your business be careful about the personal information you include.

As with all social media, blogging is about engaging with other people as your customers will enjoy seeing and reading what you've been doing - after all people buy products and services from businesses they like and won't bother with those they dislike or don't know much about. Remember that blogging shouldn't be a chore, and that it will add to your online presence in terms of visitor numbers, interaction with potential customers and hopefully generating more business.

YouTube

This is also a great way to show off your products as well as sharing any hints, tips and expertise with viewers. You don't need an expensive camera, but it's a good idea to use a tripod to stop the dreaded camera shake.

There are lots of other social media you can explore, and it's a good idea to experiment with a few and see what works for you. Social media can be very time-consuming and it's better to concentrate on one or two areas and have a really good presence than spread yourself too thinly and disappoint your visitors.

Next month brings the final instalment in this series - setting up your own website.

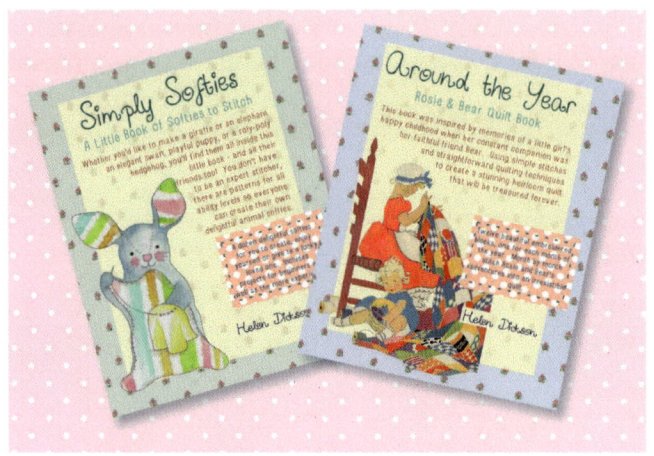

Two free books when you subscribe to the Bustle & Sew e-Magazine

www.bustleandsew.com/magazine

Celebration Cake

I think this might perhaps be my favourite pattern in this month's magazine. After all .. Celebration … cake … applique and bunting - what could be nicer!?

Again I've mounted mine within a recycled picture frame, but you could just as easily mount it on an artist's canvas block. My frame was a little taller and narrower than standard but a 16" x 12" frame or block would work well.

You will need:

- 12" x 16" canvas block or picture frame
- 7" x 16" rectangle cotton fabric for bottom part of background
- 14" x 16" rectangle cotton fabric for top part of background
- 9" x 5" cotton fabric for cake stand
- 8" x 6" brown marl felt for cake
- 8" x 4" cream felt for topping/filling
- 8" x 4" red cotton fabric for jam and strawberries
- Assorted scraps of printed cotton fabric for bunting and applique "cake"
- 24" narrow cream ribbon
- Stranded cotton floss in dark blue, pink, green and variegated colours
- White cotton fabric suitable for printing on - the word "celebrate" is printed onto fabric either directly using special fabric you can purchase for bubblejet printers or using transfer paper.
- Temporary fabric marker pen
- Cream and mid-grey thread
- Embroidery foot for your sewing machine
- Bondaweb
- If using picture frame 12" x 16" (to fit back of frame) low loft wadding and PVA craft glue
- If using an artist's canvas block you will need a staple gun to attach your design to the back of the block.

Prepare your frame:

If you're using a picture frame dissasemble it and dispose of the glass safely. Glue the wadding to the back of the frame (the side the picture sits on) using your PVA glue and leave to dry.

Applique:

- With a ¼" seam join the two pieces of background fabric along a longer edge. Press seam open to minimise bulk at the reverse of the design.
- Place your block or back onto the centre of your background fabric and draw around it with your temporary fabric marker pen. This will help you position your design.
- Transfer the design to your fabric using your preferred method. I transferred the whole design, but you could simply build up the shape by following the templates/photographs and just transfer the words "let's" and "CAKE" ready to embroider.
- Trace the cake stand shape onto the paper side of your Bondaweb and cut out roughly. Fuse to the reverse of your fabric and cut out carefully using long smooth strokes. Position on background fabric either following the design you transferred or 3 ½" above the line you drew marking the base of your frame/block
- When you're happy with the positioning fuse into place with a hot iron.

- With your temporary fabric marker pen draw on lines for edge of top, and decoration on pedestal, then, with grey thread in your needle and cream in your bobbin and your embroidery foot stitch over these lines going around twice - don't be too neat as you want a sort of scribbled effect, a bit like pencil lines.

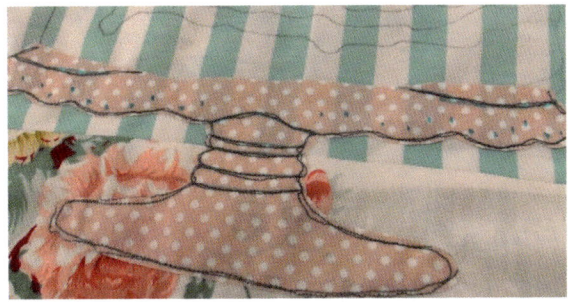

- Tracing and cutting the applique shapes in the same way start to build up the cake shapes from the bottom - allowing a little extra at the top of each shape so that the next shape will overlap it. Stitch each shape into place as you go.

- When you get to the strawberries cut the ones at the back from a single piece of felt then superimpose the two front ones - this saves messing around with very small pieces of felt.

- Applique the word "CAKE" in the same way.

- Add embroidered details using two strands of floss. The text and the two legs holding the word "celebrate" are worked in satin stitch, the strawberry stalks and leaves in straight stitch and the thread from which the letters hang in back stitch.

- Print the letters of the word "CELEBRATE" and applique to the thread going around each letter just once.

- Remove any temporary lines remaining and press your work on the reverse.

- Cut 7 triangles of fabric, each measuring 2" long and 1 ¾" wide at the top for the bunting flags and machine stitch them to the cream ribbon.

- If using picture frame insert work into frame and secure at back with tape or pins.

- If using canvas block mount your work and secure at back with staples.

- Add strings of bunting diagonally across top corners as shown securing with glue, tape or pins.

- Your picture is now finished.

Princess and the Pea

Design is actual size and also reversed to suit your preferred method of transfer and for tracing onto your Bondaweb

Hare in a Hat

Templates are actual size

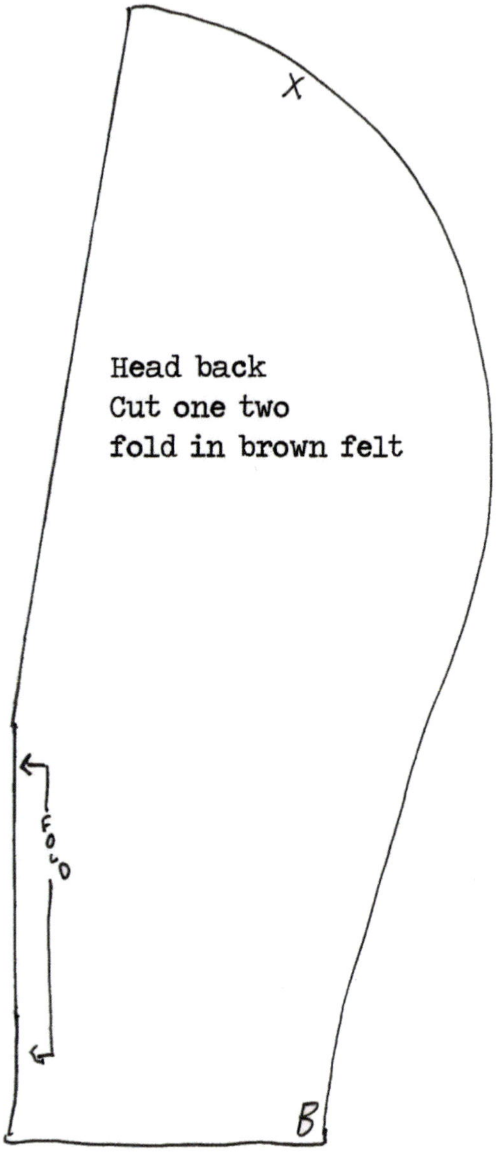

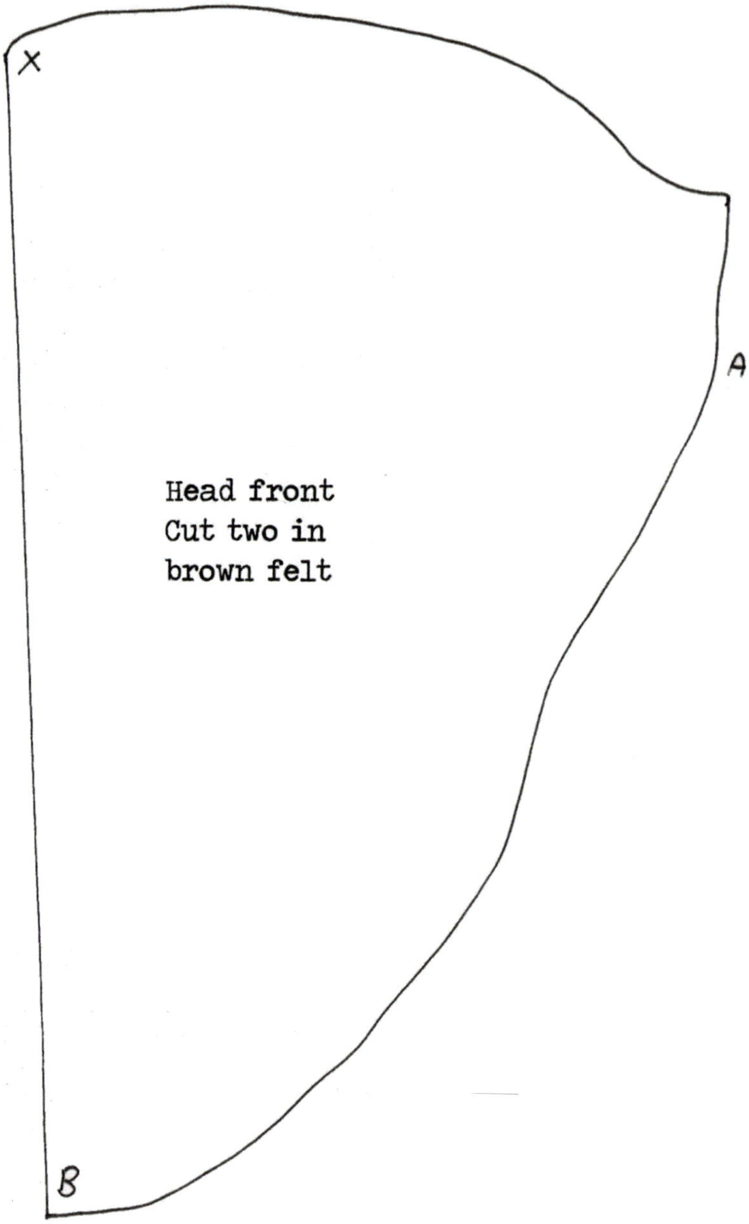

Head back
Cut one two
fold in brown felt

X

fold

B

Head front
Cut two in
brown felt

X

A

B

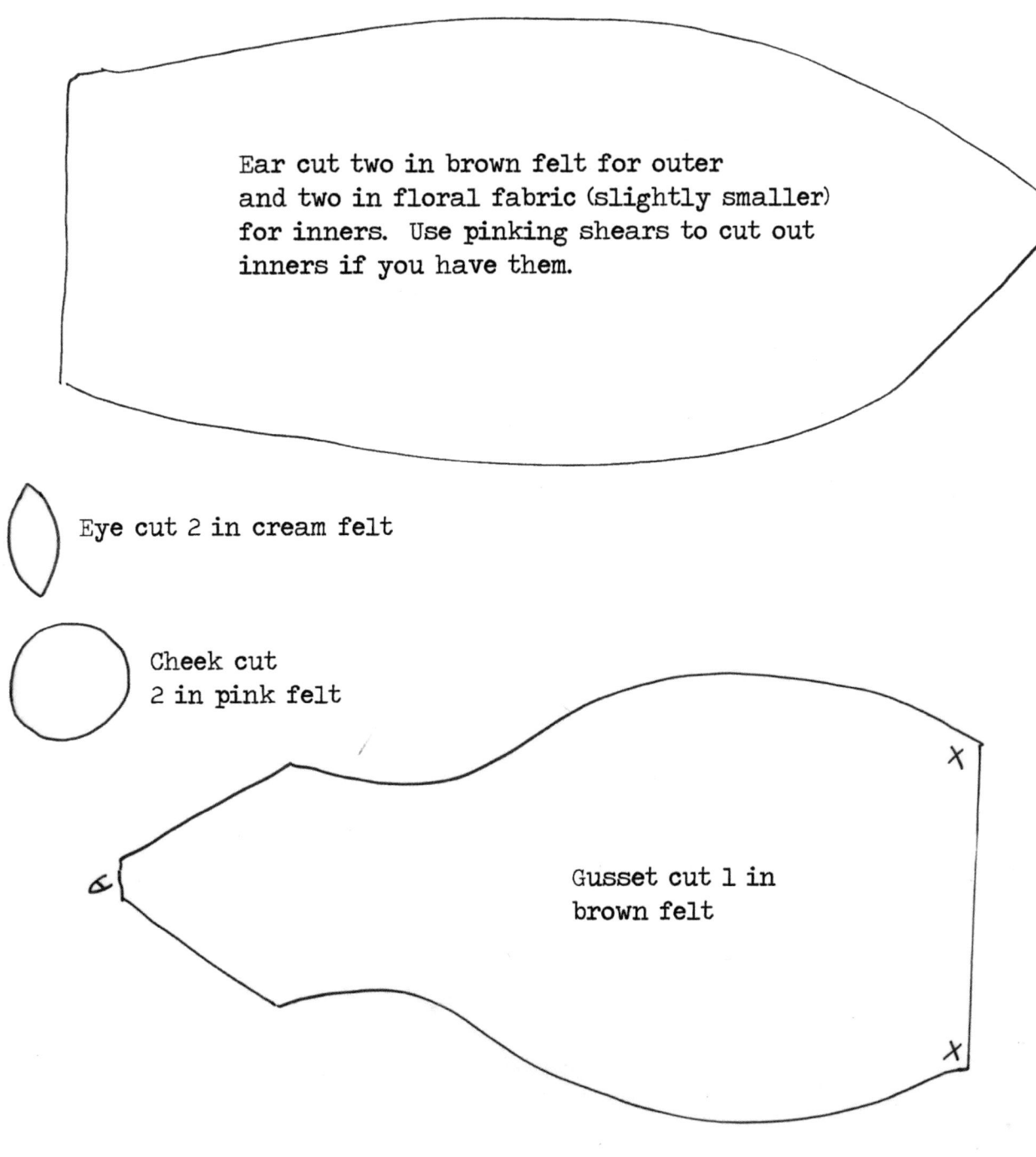

Ear cut two in brown felt for outer and two in floral fabric (slightly smaller) for inners. Use pinking shears to cut out inners if you have them.

Eye cut 2 in cream felt

Cheek cut 2 in pink felt

Gusset cut 1 in brown felt

Hat base cut one in felt of your choice

English Gardens Device Sleeve

This template is the exact size I used to make my own sleeve to fit my iPad. If you're making for a different device then you may need to resize to fit.

It is reversed for tracing the applique shapes onto your Bondaweb. On the following page it is the right way round - so you have both ways to suit your preferred method of transfer.

Friendly Fox Embroidery

Pattern is actual size and also reversed to suit your preferred method of transfer. Use the reversed pattern to trace the applique shapes onto the paper side of your bondaweb

Celebration Cake

Template is actual size and reversed for tracing onto Bondaweb. You will need to join the pieces together before tracing. The letters are also actual size and given both ways round to suit your printing method.

Note: If you are reading this in the paperback version, and want to print the letters, you will find them here:

http://bustleandsew.com/images/CelebrationCakeLetters.jpg

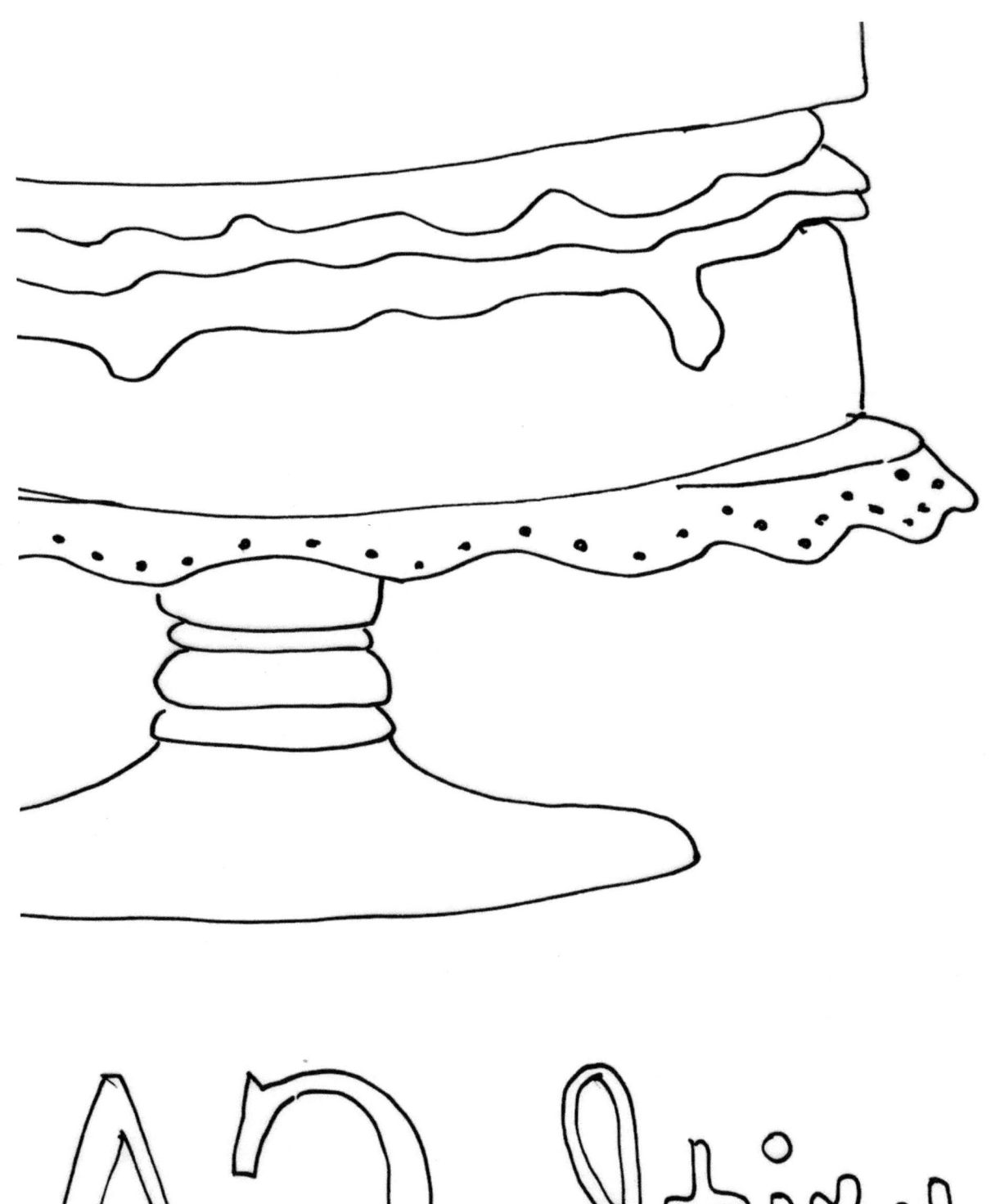

Printed in Great Britain
by Amazon.co.uk, Ltd.,
Marston Gate.